A Round Table held on July 29, 1977
and sponsored by
the American Enterprise Institute for Public Policy Research
Washington, D.C.

This pamphlet contains the edited transcript of
one of a series of AEI forums.
These forums offer a medium for
informal exchanges of ideas on current policy problems
of national and international import.
As part of AEI's program of providing opportunities
for the presentation of competing views,
they serve to enhance the prospect
that decisions within our democracy will be based
on a more informed public opinion.
AEI forums are also available on
audio and color-video cassettes.

AEI Forum 10

© 1977 by American Enterprise Institute
for Public Policy Research, Washington, D.C.
Permission to quote from
or reproduce materials in this publication is granted
when due acknowledgment is made.

ISBN 0-8447-2107-7
Library of Congress Catalog Card No. 77-81921

*Printed in the United States of America*

**J**OHN CHARLES DALY, former ABC News chief and Round Table moderator: This public policy forum, part of a series presented by the American Enterprise Institute, is concerned with the basic relationship between academia and government. The discussion is alliteratively entitled "Professors, Politicians, and Public Policy."

Our panel, professors all, is a splendid mix, with two members now serving as United States senators, another a former solicitor general of the United States, and the fourth, an editor who has described himself as a journalist, or at best, a man of letters.

To establish a broad base for the dialogue, gentlemen, will you in turn briefly address the question: How deeply has the academic community affected government policy?

DANIEL PATRICK MOYNIHAN, United States senator (Democrat, New York): Sam Hayakawa and I agreed ahead of time that we would say *academia*.

MR. DALY: I knew I was going to have a problem. I must confess that I asked Professor Hayakawa how to pronounce that silly word. I have been pronouncing it four different ways all day, and I doubt very much I will have it right before the night is out, but I will try.

SENATOR MOYNIHAN: You can remember the pronunciation by thinking of academia nuts. [Laughter and applause.] About your question, it may be that we are not the best

1

people to ask. I think of the occasion when Oscar Wilde was taken to view Niagara Falls. He stared a moment, then said, "You know, it would be more impressive if it flowed the other way." [Laughter.]

From the time of the church fathers, academia has influenced the whole experience of government in the West. Adam Smith was a professor. In our time, academia has affected the personnel of politics. I was a member of the cabinet of President Ford, a solid, sensible, serious man. The only time I ever doubted him was at a cabinet meeting one morning. Looking around, I saw six professors at that rather small table of fourteen chairs. The secretary of state was a professor. The secretary of defense was a professor. The attorney general was a professor. The secretary of labor was a professor. The secretary of agriculture was a professor. The U.S. permanent representative at the United Nations was a professor.

This is new, and it affects the way people think about politics. It is the big change from the long hegemony of lawyers in American political life.

IRVING KRISTOL, resident scholar, American Enterprise Institute: In the nineteenth century, in the frontier towns of the West, a professor was defined as the man who played the piano in the bordello. [Laughter.] And the old western movies on the late, late show often have a cowboy coming into the bar, telling the piano player to play something, and addressing him as professor. This suggests that professors were not highly regarded when it came to doing serious things, though they obviously had skills, say at the piano, that the average American did not have.

That has changed radically in the past century or century and a half. Together with their satellite group, the media, professors today are the only sector of our society which claims the right to define the public interest. Every other sector in the society is now defined as a special interest. [Laughter.]

2

Professors are the ones who know what the public interest is, and they have gained credibility in terms of their power to define it.

SAMUEL I. HAYAKAWA, United States senator (Republican, California): To take the matter outside our own country, it seems to me that one of the problems of communism is that it is a dictatorship of intellectuals and professors. It is essentially a dictatorship of people who have read the sacred books, who know the answers to all problems of public interest, and who, therefore, are able to define what is good for everybody—far better than the hardware man, the blacksmith, the accountant, or the realtor could. Professors know their way around in the world of ideas, the world of moral values.

In this country, we have not gone as far as the Communist nations in elevating the ideologue, the theoretician, to a lofty place in society. But, as Senator Moynihan described, we were getting there pretty fast with President Ford's cabinet. President Lyndon Johnson's respect for professors was extraordinarily exaggerated, but, perhaps, that is because he went to Southwest Texas Teachers College. [Laughter.]

I say please don't be in awe of professors.

ROBERT H. BORK, Chancellor Kent professor of law, Yale Law School: Professors are probably the single most influential class in terms of public policy in the United States, and that is not only because they man administrations. I know that Senator Moynihan has manned the last half dozen administrations in this country. [Laughter.]

As verbalists, professors are skilled in ideas and are quite articulate. And that happens to be a very intimidating and very influential style in this society.

It is demonstrable that our foreign policy would be quite different were it not for the influence of the professoriate. The outcome of the Vietnam War was heavily influ-

3

enced by the attitude of the campuses. In domestic policy, we have been moving in directions that the professoriate has wanted us to move for a long time.

Mr. Daly: Ladd and Lipset, authors of *The Divided Academy*, quote President John Adams as saying in 1798, "I really begin to think, or rather to suspect, that learned academies not under the immediate inspection and control of government have disorganized the world, and are incompatible with social order." Now that we are two hundred years old as a nation, does our history show that to be true?

Senator Moynihan: Adams's son, John Quincy, was Boylston professor of rhetoric at Harvard before he became President. I had thought that I was the first Harvard professor to become a senator. I was the second.

John Adams was speaking of the universities of clerics. The role of the cleric, from the Middle Ages and the Christian and Hebraic tradition, was an academic intellectual one. This is a problem for Sam Hayakawa.

In terms of the influence of people whose main interest is ideology and whose normal locus is the university, in what way is the twentieth century university different from, say, Cambridge University in the seventeenth century?

Senator Hayakawa: We have often had government by soldiers as a ruling class, and, of course, landowners have governed in other times of world history. And sometimes there were combinations of landowners and soldiers and farmers. But, as Professor Bork says, our culture has become predominantly verbal, and the verbalist has perhaps more than his due share of influence, as opposed to, say, the seafarer, or the aviator, or the engineer, or the physician—people who do things with something other than words or in addition to words. I am not sure that it is an entirely good thing for a culture. As a semanticist, I have spent pretty much of my career in the study of words and their influence on human affairs, and I have come to distrust those whose lives are exclusively preoccupied with them.

PROFESSOR KRISTOL: The big difference between the academy today and what we might call the clerisy of yesterday is the convergence between the world of thought and the world of action over the last century. The professors of a hundred years ago were assumed to be scholars and teachers who lived pretty much in an ivory tower, and, in fact, were supposed to live in an ivory tower. It was assumed that they had great knowledge of certain things, but this knowledge was not necessarily a good guide to practical action. Rarely were they turned to for guidance on matters of public policy. As moralists and philosophers, they were influential in general terms, as Adam Smith was, but it was not until quite late in the nineteenth century that they were first taken seriously as "experts."

In our day, of course, professors are taken very seriously on public policy. Every professor in the United States is convinced that his opinions ought to be sought out on such matters. If a professor is told that he lives in an ivory tower, he denies it indignantly. If we suggest to him that he ought to live in an ivory tower, he thinks we are mad.

Some of the 600,000 professors in this country are genuinely interested in teaching and scholarship, but the major interest of a considerable number of them is worldly affairs. They want to help run the world.

PROFESSOR BORK: I suppose the largest single factor in the increase of influence of the academic world is the explosion in its size. When the number of professors was small, they did not think of themselves as a class, with special interests and influence. The number of professors and students has increased so much that they now have achieved a critical mass. They feel themselves to be a distinct group, with distinct interests of their own. They press their attitudes upon society, with a suggestion that if the society does not accept their ideas, it is morally deficient.

PROFESSOR KRISTOL: Over the past decade or so, I have noticed that people, especially Presidents, have fallen into the habit of referring to all college professors as Doctor. That was not the case before, and I do not know whether Henry Kissinger started it or Pat Moynihan started it. [Laughter.]

These days every college professor is automatically called Doctor. Even I am called Doctor, though I do not have a doctorate.

SENATOR MOYNIHAN: I came to Washington under President Kennedy, and I kept my doctorate a secret. Nobody knew. I worked for Arthur Goldberg for five years, and he was on the Supreme Court before he found out I had a Ph.D. I thought it was best he not know. [Laughter.]

Bob Bork has said something important about the presumption of academics and professors that they know something other people ought to accept. In a democracy, there is a problem when a large number of persons, who would define themselves as professionals, are in positions of leadership. It is kind of a play on words, *professor-profession*. Our society has paid little attention to the development of the professions. The history of trade unions fills libraries, but there are few books on how the American Medical Association became the only authority on cutting somebody open, or how the bar association began.

The professions profess to know things other people do not know. Only they can admit others to their society, and outsiders may not question their standards.

There is a move to professionalize everything— undertakers want to be a profession. But a member of a real profession can look somebody in the eye and say, "You think you know, but you don't know—I know. And that is what it says here on this certificate on the wall—that I know and you don't." That is not a relationship of a democratic politician to a democratic citizen. It is different, isn't it?

MR. DALY: Professor Kristol, I think you defined an intellectual as a man who speaks with general authority about a subject on which he has no particular competence. [Laughter.]

SENATOR MOYNIHAN: Now, wait just a second. [Laughter.] The competence within the professions is very real. The important point is that the society has accepted the idea of their competency. Society accepts the idea that only a dentist should tell a man that he can be a dentist.

PROFESSOR BORK: I think Pat Moynihan is missing something, though. A professional with a degree on the wall, which says he is qualified to talk about law, if he is a professor, will talk about everything else but law, and expect others to listen to him anyway. There are linguists who know all about the war in Vietnam. The one I am referring to is not here this evening. [Laughter.] And there are economists who know all about moral values. They are listened to because they are professors.

SENATOR MOYNIHAN: The primal profession in our society was the clerisy, the church. It gave way to the lawyer, and the lawyer spoke on a wide range of subjects.

PROFESSOR BORK: That is surely justified. [Laughter.]

PROFESSOR KRISTOL: No, no. I think Pat Moynihan has touched on an important point. The lawyer was not given credibility as an expert in other matters because he had studied law books, but because it was assumed that the practice of law had brought him a great deal of worldly wisdom. He knew a great deal about the affairs of men, and, above all, he knew how to adjudicate quarrels—which is the essence of politics.

PROFESSOR BORK: More than that, there was a time when the knowledge professions that have proliferated recently did not exist. The only profession of verbalists was the law.

PROFESSOR KRISTOL: We are getting at something terribly important—the convergence of the realms of thought and of action. In the United States today, most professors of international relations genuinely believe they know how to run American foreign policy. And most professors of economics genuinely believe they know how to run the economy and would very much like to have the chance to prove it. The university of yesteryear did not have such people for the most part. For the most part, it had people who thought they were educating. They might want to educate public opinion in certain ways, but they did not have the feeling that they were peculiarly suited to run things.

MR. DALY: In an article in the June 14 *Wall Street Journal*, you wrote that what was striking about the economics of Charles Schultze and the Council of Economic Advisers was their "candid avowal of intellectual bankruptcy. Their fiscal and monetary policies neither stimulate the economy nor slow down the rate of inflation; they freely confess to not knowing why; and more and more frequently, they are talking softly about price controls as 'a last resort.' "

It occurs to me, speaking as a layman, that our economic policies, beginning with Franklin Delano Roosevelt and Keynes, came out of a marriage of the academic world and government. Was it a bad marriage?

PROFESSOR KRISTOL: That is a good question. But, first of all, Charles Schultze certainly would not make such a candid avowal. I was taking a bit of literary license by interpreting his remarks as representing a candid avowal. [Laughter.] Heads of the Council of Economic Advisers do not admit to intellectual bankruptcy, or to not knowing what to do. However, the point is the economy of our country is in the hands

8

of professionals who do not know what to do, but, nevertheless, have the only professional authority to do anything. I think it was George Bernard Shaw who said that it was only after 1905 that doctors started to do more good than harm to their patients.

SENATOR MOYNIHAN: No, no.

PROFESSOR KRISTOL: Wasn't it George Bernard Shaw?

SENATOR MOYNIHAN: It is still a dispute in medicine at what point in time the random patient with the random disease turned out to be better off meeting the random doctor than otherwise.

Some say 1910 and others say 1921. They learned a lot from their mistakes, though.

But Shaw did say in "Maxims for Revolutionists" in *The Revolutionist's Handbook and Pocket Companion*, "He who can, does. He who cannot, teaches." [Laughter.]

PROFESSOR KRISTOL: Nevertheless, doctors were a profession prior to 1905, and the fact that they may have done more harm than good on a randomized basis did not stop them from being doctors with a certain claim to expertise. In regard to economists, I have a dreadful feeling that we may be at 1903 or 1893. [Laughter.]

They are the only experts we have, but I am not at all sure they are doing more good than harm. They have a lot of theories, and they are sure their theories are worthwhile and important. I am not so sure the world has improved much since we began being governed by economic theories rather than by men of experience using some common sense.

SENATOR MOYNIHAN: Irving, that is not so. Would you like to work at the average hourly wages in the garment industry of 1903?

9

PROFESSOR KRISTOL: What does that have to do with economic theory?

SENATOR MOYNIHAN: We are talking about the advance of knowledge which has shaped our whole lives. Its fundamental features are the great distrust of technology that has come out of academia, and some measure of managing it.

There are some nuts among the professoriate, but much the greater number are just people who have the security of "tenure." As a matter of fact, most of the best professors, when asked really difficult questions, say, "I don't know."

And who first pointed out that not everything is known in economics? Herb Stein said that—in impeccable academese—when he was chairman of the Council of Economic Advisers. A couple of years later, Arthur Burns, chairman of the Federal Reserve Board, went before a committee of Congress and put it in an indirect way. He said, "Things aren't working the way they used to work."

PROFESSOR KRISTOL: The question is whether they used to work the way they used to work, but never mind. [Laughter.]

There are good academics, who do not go around saying they know when, in fact, they know they do not. In fact, some of us are making a profession out of explaining how much we and others do not know. That is known as critical sociology.

PROFESSOR BORK: We may be leading up to the question of whether the professoriate has characteristic viewpoints, whether there is a general outlook of intellectuals and—I am not going to try that word—

MR. DALY: I wish I hadn't.

PROFESSOR BORK: —and academicians as a class. And that is wider than economics or law. The book by Ladd and Lipset, to which Mr. Daly referred, shows what we all know from common observation—that professors, particularly those from the most prestigious universities, tend rather strongly to be left liberals and to prefer more government regulation in economics and social matters. In foreign policy, they tend to be less aggressive or less likely to defend aggressive American actions overseas. The tendency of verbalists to assume expertise they do not have may be less important than the fact that the pressure, the outlook, the verbalization is primarily in one direction.

MR. DALY: In *The Divided Academy*, the authors conclude that the faculty political orientation differs greatly in the different academic disciplines. The authors notice the difference between the political views of professors of social studies and professors of engineering, for instance.

SENATOR MOYNIHAN: There is a hierarchy of professors along those lines. Geologists and agronomists are fundamentally conservative. At the other end of the scale are the sociologists.

SENATOR HAYAKAWA: This deals with the fundamental distinction between human beings. There are people whose lives revolve around the handling of symbols, words. They are the intellectuals, the preachers, the lawyers, the media people. They are the people who speculate in grain futures without ever harvesting a bushel of grain. They are verbalists, the symbol handlers.

Then there are the other people, the thing handlers. They can be engineers, whose words or diagrams must be ultimately validated in a bridge that stands up or in a building that sustains its own weight. They can be pastry chefs— whatever words they may read in a cookbook have to be validated in an actual production, in a nonverbal production.

Both classes use words and symbols. There is one class

whose words are ultimately validated in a nonverbal event, as in the case of a farmer or an agronomist or an engineer or geologist. Then there are those like philosophers, sociologists, and English majors like me and lawyers like you. Their words do not come under the discipline of a load that shifts and turns over the truck before the driver knows it. Their words are not subject to the discipline of the great steamship that wanders off course because of factors that were neglected in a lecture on navigation.

This is the great division. If there is something wrong with our culture, it is not just in academia. It is in the whole class of symbol manipulators who rule the world. William Rusher was groping for this when he said that people could be divided into producers and nonproducers. As a verbalist, he had to classify himself as a nonproducer, along with other intellectuals and the media people. The media people do not partake of the events—they read ticker tapes, about them, and they read telegrams and news releases. Then they sit wisely in front of a typewriter or a television camera and explain the world to everybody, without, for example, having put out the fire that they are reporting, without having started it—without having the checkpoints in the nonverbal world.

If there is any amelioration of the condition under which so many of us suffer from the barrage of windbags all over the place—and I refer to ourselves as well as the media people, the people who handle the symbols—it seems to me we all require discipline in rooting our ultimate experience in the nonverbal world. This is why I have always felt that all of us in the verbal professions ought to take up something nonverbal.

SENATOR MOYNIHAN: Sam, how can you say that? The only things that matter are symbols. Everybody knows that. [Laughter.]

SENATOR HAYAKAWA: I know, I know.

SENATOR MOYNIHAN: How does *St. John* begin—In the beginning was the word? Symbols are what rule our lives.

SENATOR HAYAKAWA: If you go to a restaurant, in the beginning is the word—the word on the menu.

PROFESSOR KRISTOL: I want to elaborate on what Sam Hayakawa was saying, because I think he has put his finger on it exactly. By the way, it is interesting that we seem to be using the terms *professors* and *intellectuals* interchangeably. As Robert Nisbet once pointed out, anyone who wanted to criticize a professor seventy-five years ago called him an intellectual, and anyone who wanted to criticize an intellectual, called him academic. They were two different worlds. The intellectuals were not in universities—they were in Greenwich Village or somewhere else. They were not supposed to be in universities. But there has been a merger. Academicians have taken over the attitude of intellectuals, and, of course, intellectuals are now located on campuses.

Both professors and intellectuals today are rationalists. They believe that anyone who knows the right theory can bake the right cake, and that practical experience in baking cakes is not important. They think having the right theory of politics is more important than practical wisdom about the governance of men and women.

This is what Michael Oakeshott calls the rationalist's fallacy, that if we know the theory, we also know the practice. But the world of fact, the world of reality is very recalcitrant to theory. It reminds me of the famous story of the Israeli young man who tried to volunteer for the navy. They asked him if he could swim. He said, "No, but I know the theory of it."

There is a difference, and many of the important things in this world cannot be learned systematically. They can only be learned by practical experience, by having a sense, as a cook has a sense, of just how much to put in and how much not to put in. Government is a practical art, not a theoretical

13

art. One of the problems we suffer from at the moment is the infusion into government of political science, political theory,—

SENATOR HAYAKAWA: Sociology.

PROFESSOR KRISTOL: —sociology, and the extrusion of practical wisdom.

SENATOR MOYNIHAN: Government is altogether a theoretical art. It deals fundamentally with symbols, and it is the only thing people really care about. It is the only thing they will die for. It is the thing they most live for. And that troubles you, Irving, and I don't blame you for being troubled. [Laughter.]

SENATOR HAYAKAWA: What you say is very beautiful, Pat. You have a theory of housing for the poor, and we have lots of wonderful theoreticians who have lots of theories about housing for the poor. That is why we still have a housing problem for the poor. [Laughter.]

PROFESSOR KRISTOL: I agree with Pat Moynihan, that the symbols of authority are of ultimate importance, but the symbols of authority are not the same as governance. Acceptance of the symbols of authority permits a man to govern, but once he has that permission, he has the job to do.

One of the things that has happened—not just in the United States but also in Western Europe, in Africa, in Asia—is the infusion of various theories into the world of practice and the depreciation of practical wisdom, of traditional wisdom. It is no longer good enough to say the reason we should do it this way is that we have always done it this way and it seems to work. That is no longer acceptable as a reason for doing something, and yet it probably is the best reason for doing something in the world.

PROFESSOR BORK: Pat's point may be that, unfortunately,

reality can often be perceived only through theory and symbols, and we must try to perceive that reality through, for example, economics. The practical cook may produce disasters, so the question is, Who is the best theorist? The difficulty is that in the symbol world of the verbalist, there is no external discipline. If the building falls down, it can be attributed to some nontheoretical factor, or to the fact that the theory was not taken far enough. But there is no escape from using theorists and verbalists in these matters.

PROFESSOR KRISTOL: Theorists and verbalists do have a function. I do not mean to ridicule them. They have a very important role to play in shaping our general way of looking at the world. But that is different from actually intervening in public policy and shaping particular issues in particular spheres. Obviously, educators teach people to view the world in a certain way. Professors and intellectuals have that function. Whether they execute it well or not is another matter, but no one can take away that particular function from them. They teach our children how to look at the world. I think they should be doing it better than they are. On the other hand, that function is not the same as the governance of men or the governance of affairs.

PROFESSOR BORK: I tried to introduce a note before, and nobody picked up. I will try it one more time.

PROFESSOR KRISTOL: Maybe it wasn't a very good one. [Laughter.]

PROFESSOR BORK: Either it wasn't a very good one, or my audience wasn't up to it. [Laughter.]

It is this: We are talking about a class of people which, we seem to agree, is quite important and which has problems because it is not subject to external discipline. But I wonder if it is not true, that this class of people has distinctive public policy biases and, therefore, tends to move our public policy in a particular direction.

SENATOR HAYAKAWA: I believe it does tend to move public policy in certain directions. It moves people in the direction of often being overly enchanted with a body of theory, so that they go in the direction of what Karl Popper calls utopianism. This class draws a mental picture of a beautiful, beautiful world it would like to move reality to. Insofar as we have utopian elements in our social planning—and social planning itself involves a certain kind of utopianism, we try to impose a map on the territory and make the territory conform to it, rather than the other way around. Gosh, I am talking like a general semanticist.

SENATOR MOYNIHAN: You are talking like a professor with one of a range of views professors have about how to run government properly, which is: Don't do too much.

You cite Karl Popper. I studied with him in the London School of Economics. You know, the English have a verb which is conjugated "*I* am Oxford, *you* are Cambridge, *he* is the London School of Economics." [Laughter.]

I studied with Popper, and I read *The Open Society and Its Enemies.* Popper is very much anti-Platonic, very much pro-Aristotelian—two professors, Plato and Aristotle, as are Professor Popper and Professor Moynihan. Here is evidence of a degradation in the professoriate.

In the end, the important things are really questions and professors will be asked about them. Let me ask a really serious question. What is the difference between a dog dying and a human fetus dying? Is there one?

PROFESSOR KRISTOL: You are asking professors this question?

SENATOR MOYNIHAN: Professors will end up answering it.

PROFESSOR KRISTOL: That is another matter.

SENATOR MOYNIHAN: Professors will end up answering it. A

professor writing in *Science* recently said that the dog is a noble and accomplished and sensitive creature.

PROFESSOR KRISTOL: And they are more grateful to their masters.

SENATOR MOYNIHAN: And they are not much different.

PROFESSOR KRISTOL: From children?

SENATOR MOYNIHAN: And yet other professors have told us there is a profound difference. These are important questions, and they are not readily answerable. So we accommodate ourselves through symbols, and we have to live with them.

PROFESSOR KRISTOL: Sam Hayakawa has uttered a key word—*utopianism*. One of the historical products of the explosion of the modern academy that Bob Bork referred to has been a strong element of utopianism in our society.

We had a wonderful instance of this only a few weeks ago when the President of the United States said on television that life is unfair. Now, I do not know any taxi driver in the United States who would disagree with him. Nevertheless, a lot of college graduates became very upset because he said life is unfair. They have figured out that life is not supposed to be unfair, and, by God, if we give them the chance, they will see to it that it is not unfair.

MR. DALY: Professor Bork, you raised an issue about the spread of education. Has the spread of education, particularly university education, decreased or increased the acceptance of our society's institutions?

PROFESSOR BORK: It probably has decreased the moral authority of the institutions of the society. The intellectual class generally tends to be highly critical of traditional institutions and tends to, as somebody said, actively unfit the students for their future environment. In fact, some members of this class think that is their function, to make students dissatisfied with their future environment. As Lionel Trilling said, that is not only an adversary intention, it is also a subversive intention. We can observe a flattening of the American institutional landscape, in part because of the attitudes inculcated in the university and carried on by the university's allies, the media and the clergy. In that sense I think the influence has been quite harmful to traditional institutions and values.

SENATOR MOYNIHAN: Didn't Lionel Trilling write that essay on the adversary culture in 1947?

PROFESSOR BORK: About that, yes.

SENATOR MOYNIHAN: Are we in a cycle or are we in a fixed condition, a stasis? The academic who has had the greatest political influence in this century surely was Woodrow Wilson. Professor Wilson became President, and, surely, in the most extraordinary way he confirmed the basic American ideas of the time. He was scarcely hostile to what was established. His intention was neither subversive, nor adversary.

Need we continue in the phase that started in the 1930s? Academia was supportive of institutions until the Great Depression, and the movement into them of ethnic groups previously on the outside. May academia now not begin to celebrate the "establishment"? What is the brightest think tank in Washington? The American Enterprise Institute. Radical, it is not. Subversive, certainly not. [Laughter.]

PROFESSOR KRISTOL: This has to be said as an addendum to Bob Bork's point, which is essentially correct. One of the functions of intellectuals and education is to alienate students from their society. A student is supposed to gain a certain detachment from his society, but it is supposed to be an intellectual detachment.

SENATOR MOYNIHAN: Irving, that is not so. What did Joseph Schumpeter say of capitalism? He said that capitalism is a process of "creative destruction." It destroys the usefulness of last year's automobiles, as well as last year's ideas. Some of you tend to dissociate this particular role of the academia from the larger culture. Schumpeter would probably say that there was never a more capitalist institution than the anti-establishment university. It is the essence of the capitalist mode. If you do not like that, try feudalism, try socialism, but don't try enterprise, because enterprise keeps saying no.

PROFESSOR BORK: That is a good point.

SENATOR HAYAKAWA: Woodrow Wilson had many of the characteristics of the intellectual, and the worst one of all was this utopianism we are talking about. He drove the world towards an unrealizable dream and was terribly disillusioned when he found it was unrealizable. It is a characteristic story of—

SENATOR MOYNIHAN: Of professors or Presbyterians? [Laughter.]

SENATOR HAYAKAWA: Perhaps both.

PROFESSOR BORK: As Irving Kristol said, it is the characteristic function of professors and other intellectuals to question the status quo and to produce intellectual alienation in students. If that were the only explanation of the attitudes we see in professors, then we would expect to see the universities severely questioning the welfare state and the regulatory state and undercutting the status quo. But that is not the case. They are not opposed to the status quo; they are opposed to particular institutions.

PROFESSOR KRISTOL: A good education should have an alienating consequence of a kind. I want to defend the notion that education should liberate the young person to understand the limitations of his society as compared with previous societies. Only then can he read the Greek authors and understand that they were greater than any playwright we have had in our century. But that is intellectual liberation, a private liberation for private consumption. It was not assumed at Harvard in the 1880s that this liberation would then send students out into the society to overturn it.

SENATOR MOYNIHAN: Irving, that was what they did in that decade. At Harvard in the 1880s, they wanted to go out and Christianize America at last. There was a great revival.

PROFESSOR KRISTOL: There was a changing society.

MR. DALY: In 1873, Whitelaw Reid said that a function of the American scholar in politics was to give intellectual leadership to radicals, which bears out what Senator Moynihan said.

SENATOR MOYNIHAN: I want to speak up for academia because I will never get back to it and I long for it. It does preserve. It preserves Aeschylus, and it preserves Plato, and it preserves Trilling. Tell me one damn thing that General Motors has ever preserved. Every year a new world is begun, and the past is over, has to be changed, got rid of.

PROFESSOR BORK: Do you want General Motors to preserve the car model of 1910?

SENATOR MOYNIHAN: I thought 1925 was a good year. [Laughter.]

PROFESSOR BORK: Your argument might lead to the conclusion that General Motors has moved on since 1925, but the academic world has not. They are still producing that old, bad model up there in Cambridge. [Laughter.]

SENATOR MOYNIHAN: I went to the City College of New York,

and Irving Kristol did, too, and we don't have to apologize for that. Here you are in the American Enterprise Institute. You are in the vortex of the destruction of values; to wit, whatever you had last year, you must be dissatisfied with and get something new.

PROFESSOR KRISTOL: That is a valid point. Capitalism is destructive of values. It is no accident that the criticism of society made by professors, for instance, and their recommendations for public policy never suggest less power, prestige, or authority for professors.

As our conflict of interest laws are now defined, it is almost impossible for a businessman or a trade unionist to take a job in government. The one group who can take jobs in government are professors. After a job in government, they come right back to the university. There are no conflicts of interest. Is it an accident that this is the way the conflict of interest laws are being promulgated?

SENATOR MOYNIHAN: In the Senate, we recently instituted draconian restraints on how much money any senator could earn outside from consulting, from lawyering, from doctoring, and so forth. What was the only exception, Sam?

SENATOR HAYAKAWA: Book royalties.

SENATOR MOYNIHAN: Yes. Book royalties are accepted.

PROFESSOR KRISTOL: Robert Hutchins once tried to institute a conflict of interest policy at the University of Chicago. He said in an academic community all royalties earned from textbooks and the outside lectures and consultantships should go to the university. In return he offered to pay professors much better than they had been paid, but all professors would be paid alike, regardless how popular their textbooks were. The faculty of the University of Chicago was not about to have that.

21

PROFESSOR BORK: They had a good point. We will get more scholarship if we allow some return from it, unfortunately.

SENATOR HAYAKAWA: I don't understand what is meant by "capitalism destroys values." Would someone elaborate on that? When old automobiles are destroyed, what values are destroyed?

SENATOR MOYNIHAN: In Schumpeter's analysis, the capitalist spirit appeared in the world—not least in the universities—as a rejection of the established and presumably immutable systems of the Middle Ages. This spirit says no. It says we must change, question, and argue, and it proceeds to delegitimate the authority of the church and much else, and creates its own authority. By this process of delegitimating, it created itself. But, says Schumpeter, it cannot stop there. It will then go on to delegitimate itself, and the vanguard of this process will always be the intellectuals. And, says he, the capitalist will support them, provide for them, pay for them, nurture them, because—

PROFESSOR KRISTOL: Think of the Ford Foundation.

SENATOR MOYNIHAN: —because he sees in them the essence of his own being. It is sad that he knows he is doing it to himself, but he will go on until it is all over. When it is all over, they will be quiet again, and God have mercy on them.

SENATOR HAYAKAWA: You make me awfully glad I have never read Schumpeter. [Laughter.]

PROFESSOR BORK: There is a new school of thought that all wisdom begins with Schumpeter, which is Irving Kristol's school of thought, isn't it? He calls himself a neo-Schumpeterian.

PROFESSOR KRISTOL: Never did. I can't even pronounce it.

SENATOR MOYNIHAN: I am a neo-Schumpeterian.

PROFESSOR BORK: There, that is the man. Actually, he is a quasi-Schumpeterian.

Schumpeter is quite right that the capitalist spirit, being intensely rational, does tend to quantify things, to doubt the status quo, and to destroy traditional values. The difficulty is that people do not do well without some transcendental values to believe in. The value they turn to now is the secularization of spiritual values—the equality of man, socialism, and social reform—which will probably undo capitalism.

SENATOR MOYNIHAN: That is argued. I would point to the great man himself—Schumpeter—as evidence that professors are not always dogmatic, and are capable of admitting mistakes. Schumpeter taught at Harvard at the end of his life, after he came from the Austro-Hungarian world. He said that as a young man he had three ambitions: he wished to be the world's greatest economist, the world's greatest lover, and the world's greatest horseman. But now, he said, advancing age had narrowed the horizon of opportunity, and with increasing sadness, he had to admit that he had not achieved his third ambition. [Laughter.]

MR. DALY: We have covered a lot of ground, and I am not sure all of it has been as fruitful as it might have been, and now it is time to turn to the audience and open the question and answer session. May I have the first question, please?

EVERETT BELLOWS, the Olin Corporation: I do not represent General Motors, but I do represent the American enterprise system. Since Dr. Schumpeter is not here, I have to ask Senator Moynihan, when he raised the question of values being destroyed, was he not confusing artifacts, like this year's automobile, with a value?

SENATOR MOYNIHAN: A good question. Schumpeter was enough of a Marxist to say that the interconnection between artifacts and values is very real, and that the constant changing of the one is associated with the constant changing of the other. I think that is what Schumpeter would have said.

MR. BELLOWS: What do you say?

PROFESSOR KRISTOL: You say that Schumpeter was probably right.

SENATOR MOYNIHAN: There is that wonderful striptease scene in *Pal Joey*, in which Gypsy Rose Lee is unzipping, and she says, "I was reading Schopenhauer last night," and zip, "and I think that Schopenhauer was right." [Laughter.]

PROFESSOR KRISTOL: Actually, one can phrase Schumpeter's point, and I think Pat Moynihan's point, very simply in a way that makes it almost irrefutable. A society which is constantly changing itself, and introducing new modes of thinking and new ways of looking at the world, is not very respectful of traditional values and traditional ways of doing things and of looking at the world. The effect of economic and social life on religious and academic institutions is bound to be of that nature.

HERBERT STEIN, University of Virginia: As I listened to the panel earlier, I had a feeling that their symbols were clashing. [Laughter.]

The word *professor* tends to be used to mean academic, abstract, theoretical, and impractical, while others are identified as practical men of action, men of experience, and men of the world. I have a feeling that that is an overgeneralization. The professors in government, especially at high levels, have survived the rigorous politics of the academic scene and have other practical experience, whereas many of the very practical people are living by the theories of an earlier day. Certainly, many of the bankers and businessmen undertook to run economic policy by obsolete theories.

However, I would like to ask Senator Moynihan about his remark that six of the fourteen people in the cabinet room were professors. Did he think that those six were more professorial and academic than the other eight?

SENATOR MOYNIHAN: Professor Stein is one of the most distinguished of the academics who have taken issue with Keynes, but he probably would not take issue with Keynes's remark that every practical businessman is the slave of some defunct economist. That is probably the case with everybody whose work stems from ideas and theories. In the main, the academics are closer to the newer ideas than those who are not academic. The newer ideas may not be better, but they are newer. Certainly, in my experience, the most practical people in government typically have been the academics. I am sorry about that.

PROFESSOR KRISTOL: But those are precisely the kinds of people who would get into government. The academic world is almost too full of people who would be very good in government. They should have been in government and in politics all along, and they find themselves quite frustrated in the academy. This is what happens when there are 600,000 professors. They are not all scholars and teachers. Some of them at the age of thirty-five suddenly realize that perhaps they should not have been professors, but it is a little late to change, so they become interested in politics.

SENATOR MOYNIHAN: But Herb Stein—who is more a novelist now than an economist [laughter]—also made the point about people who had survived. Remember Woodrow

Wilson said that he found Washington pretty simple business after Princeton University.

PROFESSOR BORK: I have just gone back to Yale after four years in Washington, and I think I may be ready for faculty politics for the first time. [Laughter.] The point is not that practical men of affairs necessarily have any better grasp of issues than academicians do, but that they have less influence than academicians do in the world and on public policy. Although I have said it before, I will say it again because I am the only one who is saying it: academics have a distinctive political slant—differing from that of the practical men of affairs—which results in a heavy influence on public policy in one direction.

PETER McPHERSON, tax lawyer, Washington, D.C.: Professor Bork has several times raised the question of bias in the academic community. Since I gather everyone agrees that this is a very important community, could the members of the panel say why there is a bias, and whether it is a long-term one.

MR. DALY: Do you want to start on that, Professor Bork?

PROFESSOR BORK: Well, I have been talking about that, so I think I will let my colleagues start on it.

PROFESSOR KRISTOL: All right. Thank you.

PROFESSOR BORK: I think I may have made a mistake. [Laughter.]

PROFESSOR KRISTOL: I don't like the term *bias*. It is the wrong word. It makes no sense to say that Rousseau was biased or Condorcet was biased. We are talking about an intellectual tradition going back well over two centuries, perhaps three centuries. The attitude toward the world today used to be the attitude, not of the professor so much, but of the intellectual class.

Those two traditions have merged. Once professors had no general ideas—they just knew a lot of Greek. But the intellectual tradition and the traditions of the academy have now become one in our society, and the attitudes that most professors have are the attitudes that intellectuals have had for three hundred years. It makes no sense to call it biased.

This attitude is rationalistic. It favors planning, as against individual freedom, let us say; it favors centralized government, as distinct from decentralized government. It is utopian in the sense that Sam Hayakawa used that word. These intellectuals believe a better world can be made out of the present world, and that they know how to do it, because that is their specialty.

So the word *bias* bothers me. If you are simply saying that academics have a way of looking at the world which predisposes them to what we call liberalism, neoliberalism, or whatever term you wish, the answer is yes, of course. There is no doubt of that.

SENATOR MOYNIHAN: I would like to hear what you and Sam Hayakawa think about the changing meaning of the word *liberal*. Academics have always been liberals. A century ago in practical government policy, *liberal* meant almost the opposite of what it means today. A century ago liberal academics wanted to reduce the influence of government; now they want to increase the influence of government. The intellectuals are holding onto that word.

But we must not overlook the diversity in academic opinion. We have a ritualistic sociology of knowledge: we know that physicists tend to be radical in politics, and engineers tend to be conservative. And that reflects something fundamental about the kinds of work they do, and about government and politics itself—about why a person's politics are the way they are. Physicists think in ways about molecules that make for radical politics. Engineers think about the same molecules in different ways, and that is absorbing and interesting. And I think you will find there are more professors of engineering than there are professors of physics.

MR. MCPHERSON: But, sir, the engineers do not generally try to tell government how it works. By and large, the engineers do not attempt to formulate general public policy nearly as much as economists and sociologists and social scientists in general, though they certainly do become involved in atomic energy policies.

SENATOR MOYNIHAN: You might be surprised who tells the government whether the B-1 bomber is better than the cruise missile. It is the engineers.

SENATOR HAYAKAWA: But that is a limited piece of advice as to a technical matter. It is true that engineers do not tell government how the world should be run, whereas intellectuals do. And engineers do not classify themselves as intellectuals but as practical men. There is a real difference in psychology there.

SENATOR MOYNIHAN: We agree on that.

SENATOR HAYAKAWA: Yes, but if someone describes himself as a practical man—and this is no derogation—he implies that the ultimate ends of society are determined by somebody else. As an engineer, he will help to achieve those ends by building certain projects and making practical suggestions. But the ultimate ends of society are determined by the philosophy departments, maybe, or the English departments or the social science departments. There are professors who do arrogate to themselves the privilege of asking what the world is for, what society is for, and to what ends we should direct society as a whole.

This is where we get into utopianism. Engineers do not do that, though every now and then one dreams up Technocracy or something like that. But those engineers are rare, are they not? On the whole, the engineer is an instrument of somebody else's ultimate decision. And this is why Plato and other philosophers say the world is properly run by philosopher kings, because they knew what ends were, whereas plumbers, engineers, cooks, barbers, et cetera, only help achieve those ends.

But all this, in a sense implies a sort of intellectual caste system that I reject from the bottom of my heart. I do not believe any one class has the right to dictate to other classes what the ends of life should be. The engineer, no less than the philosopher, has the right to determine the ends for himself, his family, his friends, and society around him.

For one class to say it has the ultimate answers is typical of the arrogance of the liberal arts and social sciences. I have been fighting that as a professor for a long, long time. And that is a great, great weakness among professors of philosophy. Why is it, for example, that in the average English department of a large university there are fifty-nine Democrats, one Republican, and forty Maoists? [Laughter.]

PROFESSOR BORK: Senator Hayakawa raised the point that I wanted to. Senator Moynihan mentioned the diversity in the academic world, but that diversity does not exist in the departments that have to do with policy in the most prestigious universities. I once had a conversation that illustrated Senator Hayakawa's point. In regard to an academic appointment, I said I was dubious about a Maoist, and I was told that we had to have a Maoist to balance the Stalinist we already had. [Laughter.]

In the policy sciences and in the professions—in the law schools, for example—we do find forty Democrats and two Republicans. I think that has implications for domestic policy, in that the academic world—in the policy sciences and in the law schools—is heavily in favor of increasing governmental intervention in society and its processes, usually in favor of greater equality and redistribution of wealth. The long-run implications are not favorable for the preservation of capitalism and a free society.

We have not mentioned another aspect—the influence of intellectuals and the academic world upon foreign affairs and foreign policy. George Orwell wrote that towards the end of World War II, when it was quite plain that the Nazis would lose and that England would win, the intellectual classes in England remained more defeatist than any other class. They talked about negotiating peace or finding some resolution with Germany, rather than carrying the war to a conclusion.

Orwell suggested—and much of our experience may suggest—that academics and intellectuals, as a class at least, have less staying power in world contests. And perhaps they have less faith that this society is ultimately better than those nations we are in a contest with. If that is true, it has serious long-run implications.

SENATOR MOYNIHAN: But Orwell also said, did he not, that this was because intellectuals had more imagination? That is what they are good at. That is their trade, having imagination. They can imagine defeat when people with less imagination cannot, thank God.

PROFESSOR BORK: They could imagine the pains one would have to go through to arrive at victory and, therefore, be less willing to put up with it.

SENATOR MOYNIHAN: Both.

PROFESSOR BORK: Whether or not one ascribes it to a good quality like imagination, it is a fact.

SENATOR MOYNIHAN: I know Orwell pretty well. In that passage, I am pretty sure he said they have more imagination.

PROFESSOR BORK: I understand that, and I will accept that,

and that is what he did say, but I don't think we are engaged in a textual argument.

SENATOR MOYNIHAN: No.

PROFESSOR BORK: If that is their characteristic, for whatever reason, and if they are a terribly influential class, then that has implications for our ability to conduct over a period of decades a contest with the Soviet Union.

DAVID SMOAK, Export-Import Bank: The case has been made by a panel of academia that capitalism is a destructive process. Cannot a case also be made that capitalism is a constructive process, that is, by replacing the old model with a better model?

SENATOR MOYNIHAN: Come on now. I raised that matter and, with respect, sir, you did not state it correctly. I referred to Schumpeter's notion of creative destruction. It contains both the thoughts you have expressed.

NORMAN ORNSTEIN, Catholic University: The panel has talked mostly as if professors had recruited themselves into the political process in the last ten or fifteen years, and as if that is why the explosion had taken place. There has not been much discussion of the politicians, the Presidents, and others bringing professors into the public policy process. President Kennedy brought Professor, Doctor, now Senator Moynihan, among others, in, and certainly Presidents since then have also done that. President Nixon put an emphasis on Dr. Kissinger and Dr. Schlesinger—though perhaps not Dr. Butz—and he lionized academics to some extent in the policy process. I wonder if the panel could talk about this from the viewpoint of professional politicians.

SENATOR HAYAKAWA: Well, I guess we are professional politicians now, aren't we, Pat?

MR. DALY: Yep.

31

SENATOR HAYAKAWA: We sure have brainwashed the rest of them, haven't we? [Laughter.]

MR. DALY: I think it is a good question. In both your cases, you went to the electorate, and you sought public office. I think, Professor Bork—you can correct me if I am wrong—that you were approached to join the Justice Department and ultimately become solicitor general.

PROFESSOR BORK: There was no public demand, I agree with you. [Laughter.]

MR. DALY: The question turns on whether all the intellectual community is trying to get into government or government is inducing the intellectual community to come in. What do you say, Professor Kristol?

PROFESSOR KRISTOL: I think there is a lot of the second. Politicians today do turn to the academy for two reasons. First of all, the academy is sufficiently big, with well over half a million people. There are a lot of very good, smart, competent, practical people in the academy. I think they are a minority, but they are there. It makes sense to recruit them.

In addition, however, politicians have been sufficiently influenced by the academy over the past thirty years to think that they do not understand the world unless there is a professor to explain it to them. They feel they cannot understand the world better than the professor who is the presumed expert in the subject. That is to say, politicians have been conditioned to look at the world in terms of something called problems, for which they seek something called solutions. Now, that is not the normal political way of looking at the world. The normal political way of looking at the world is that the world is what it is—full of other people—and the politician copes with them as best he can. He keeps things ticking along, hoping for the best. That is traditional, normal politics.

Once politics is defined in terms of something that is a problem to which there is presumed to be a solution, then there is a need for someone who has studied the matter. Common sense is simply not enough.

Once at a university discussion on foreign policy, I said I thought the ideal secretary of state in these last three decades would have been Mayor Daley of Chicago. My colleagues in the university just didn't understand me. I think he was ideally equipped. He knew how to get along with all sorts of people, and he knew how to knife all sorts of people when it was necessary—two very important traits. He had a very shrewd, astute—a very astute—mind. He never read a book on foreign policy, I am sure, and he may not have known where half the countries were, but that would not have mattered. I think he would have done very well.

About seven or eight months ago at a dinner, an Israeli politican—there is no secret, it was Shimon Peres, then the defense minister—uttered an extraordinarily wise remark. He was being cross-examined by a group of experts on the Middle East, and one of them asked him what would be done about East Jerusalem, the old city. He said, "That is no problem." Everyone looked at him, and the questioner asked what he meant by saying it was not a problem. Peres shrugged his shoulders and said, "In politics when you don't have a solution, you don't have a problem." [Laughter.]

Now, that is a politician speaking. It is not the sort of remark that could ever come from an academic. What has happened to our whole climate of opinion, to our whole way of looking at the world, is that we now think in terms of problems and solutions. Politicians have to go to someone who will solve the "urban problem," whatever that is.

SENATOR MOYNIHAN: I really must take issue. I think this audience will be misled if we do not insist upon a longer-term perspective.

Bob Bork has accurately described going back to Yale,

and Sam Hayakawa has asked why every department of sociology has to have fifty-nine Democrats, one Republican, and forty Maoists. Do you know why? Because it is 1977. I am not sure how it will be in the year 2017, much less how it was in the year 1817.

Irving Kristol described the practical man of politics who knows that there is no ultimate achievement, that you sail a bottomless sea to no port, and he said it brilliantly. In some considerable measure, he also said what he was taught to say by Michael Oakeshott, whom he has already introduced in our conversation. And who is Michael Oakeshott? He is the professor who succeeded Harold Laski to the chair of political philosophy at the London School of Economics. Oakeshott's view of what is proper and achievable and desirable is very different from Laski's. It takes a long time to catch up in such matters, but one can already feel in certain intermediate parts of American opinion Oakeshott's influence rising and Laski's waning. Oakeshott has been succeeded by a man with yet a third view.

There is nothing fixed or immutable in academic opinion, much less in fashion. Probably the only thing fixed is that it changes.

SENATOR HAYAKAWA: It has always seemed to me peculiar the way academic and media people, and intellectuals generally, simply do not understand Mayor Daley, for example. A wonderful example is the book *Boss*, by Mike Royko, which revealed Mayor Daley to be ruthless, corrupt, unprincipled. He formed dubious alliances with gangsters and crooked elements. He made ridiculous mistakes in grammar. [Laughter.]

Mike Royko writes for the Chicago *Daily News*, and anyone who read his book would be perfectly sure that it really finished off Mayor Daley. But shortly after it was published, Mayor Daley won the next mayoral election—at the age of seventy-three and in bad health—with his biggest majority ever. It seems to me that men of words, like Royko and other journalists or professors such as ourselves, do not understand people like Mayor Daley. I agree with Irving Kristol that he might very well have made a good secretary of state.

SENATOR MOYNIHAN: Sam, I insist that you stop that battle you had in San Francisco—don't always be punching those academics. But don't stop punching them entirely. In 1965, I became director of the Joint Center for Urban Studies of Harvard and MIT, at a time when urban policy was beginning to be an issue. I succeeded James Q. Wilson. If you had asked my predecessor on the day he left office who was the best mayor in America, he would have said Daley. If you had asked me on the day I came into office, I would have said Daley. On the day I left office I would still have said Daley, and I think the man who succeeded me would have said Daley—well, no, he was a real professor, so he would not have said Daley, but he would have got it wrong. [Laughter.]

Most of us are capable of seeing what works and what doesn't. We have eyes. Daley would have been a hell of a good secretary of state. He would have been the best secretary of state the West has had since Ernie Bevin, a man like Daley who was the first postwar foreign secretary in England and a trade unionist. Sure, there are a lot of academics who are too dumb to know how smart Daley was, but that indicates the quality of the academic, not the nature of the academic.

ALAN SELTZER, National Endowment for the Humanities research fellow at the American Enterprise Institute: Senator Moynihan, would you be more specific about the important secular values of liberal capitalist democracies that capitalism creatively destroys, or is alleged to destroy. Also, as to the process, is it capitalism that destroys such values or is it rather anti-establishment, anti-capitalist professors, who nevertheless have the capitalist orientation insofar as it involves creative destruction?

There is a second part to my question. Did Woodrow Wilson, in your view, understand these things? [Laughter.]

SENATOR MOYNIHAN: Those are good questions, and I want to make a point. The man who asked the question is clearly suspicious of the academic tendency of recent times. He is a young man, he has a beard, and he is very suspicious of all those people who are subversive of traditional values. And what is he doing? He is a fellow of the National Endowment for the Humanities here at AIE—at AEI. [Laughter.]

And that is fine, because the times they are a-changin', but not in the direction of the people who wrote that song.

Two things: You asked about values and politicians and so forth, and whether capitalism really changes them. I suppose it is really rationalism that has changed them, and rationalism is the great Marxist argument. Is rationalism a result of the steam engine or is the steam engine the result of rationalism? I don't know, but I think rationalism is the dominant force, and it can create a liberal society with maximum freedom. It can also then lead to one with a minimum of freedom.

But I will give you a prerationalist, precapitalist illustration. Prime Minister Macmillan in Great Britain was once asked about the meaning of life, and being a precapitalist, prerationalist man, he said, "Oh, my God, never ask a politician about the meaning of life. Ask your archbishop." Your archbishop. Doesn't everyone have an archbishop? Well, everyone does, but not everyone knows him. [Laughter.]

Woodrow Wilson, in the end, did not understand our system of government very well, though he was professor of government, but he did understand our values very well indeed. In the fifty years since his administration, there has never been a moment when his values have been more on display than in our present advocacy of human rights

36

around the world. It is pure Wilsonianism, which may be—well, I will stop.

MICHAEL ROBINSON, Catholic University: I have been reviewing in my head who the doctors have been, at least in the executive branch, over the last ten years. I come up with Dr. Schlesinger, Dr. Moynihan, Dr. Stein, and Dr. Butz, and I began to wonder if perhaps Professor Bork has not been misled by the Timothy Leary factor in the media. Although there may be one Republican and forty Democrats in academic departments, it is the Republican who winds up in the cabinet more often than not. If we look at the Senate—at the two members here tonight—or at the cabinet, instead of accepting what the media tell us about the liberal influence of professors on students, we see the real influence of professors on public policy has been conservative. Isn't that possible?

PROFESSOR BORK: I suppose it is possible in a given moment of time that a small set of academicians who find themselves in government might have a conservative influence. I should protest, however. Professor Moynihan keeps citing the small fraction of dissident intellectuals as if their view might become the majority view. Maybe it will, but I see no signs of that.

The impact of the academic world is heavily to the left of the general political spectrum. We receive a particular point of view from the media because of the nature of the academic world—through its writing, through its teaching, through its alliance with the media. When a journalist wants some comments on the current Supreme Court, for example, he calls constitutional law professors. It just happens that he hears very hostile comments about the Burger Court and very friendly comments about the Warren Court.

That influences the opinions of society much more than the occasional professor who winds up in a Republican administration.

37

PROFESSOR KRISTOL: Just listening to this question and answer, I suddenly realized why professors tend to get into all administrations these days. There is a relatively simple reason—namely, the importance of the media. Professors do tend to be much more articulate than businessmen or bankers, since, after all, they are lecturing to students all the time. They learn how to phrase their thoughts quickly. They learn how to respond to questions quickly. They survive on television. Businessmen tend not to be articulate. It is not necessary for them to be articulate to be highly successful. The businessman or banker does terribly on the media, and to the degree that the media has become—*have* become—more important, I suspect the academic community becomes more influential directly in government.

MR. DALY: This concludes another Public Policy Forum presented by the American Enterprise Institute for Public Policy Research. On behalf of AEI, our heartfelt thanks to the distinguished panelists, Professors Robert H. Bork and Irving Kristol, and Senators Daniel Patrick Moynihan and S. I. Hayakawa. Our thanks also to our guests and experts in the audience for their participation.

Good night.

[Applause.]